GOD
OF THE
COIN TOSS

And Other Short Stories

CHRIS CANTRELL

WESTBOW
PRESS®
A DIVISION OF THOMAS NELSON
& ZONDERVAN

Scripture quotations taken from the New American
Standard Bible® (NASB), Copyright © 1960, 1962, 1963,
1968, 1971, 1972, 1973, 1975, 1977, 1995 by The Lockman
Foundation. Used by permission. www.Lockman.org

WestBow Press books may be ordered through
booksellers or by contacting:

WestBow Press
A Division of Thomas Nelson & Zondervan
1663 Liberty Drive
Bloomington, IN 47403
www.westbowpress.com
1 (866) 928-1240

ISBN: 978-1-9736-4110-0 (sc)
ISBN: 978-1-9736-4111-7 (hc)
ISBN: 978-1-9736-4109-4 (e)

Library of Congress Control Number: 2018911516

Print information available on the last page.

WestBow Press rev. date: 10/16/2018

Whom have I in heaven **but** **You?**
And besides You, I desire nothing on earth.
My flesh and my heart may fail,
But God is the strength of my heart
and my portion forever.
For, behold, those who are far from You will perish;
You have destroyed all those who
are unfaithful to You.
But as for me, the nearness of God is my good;
I have made the Lord GOD my refuge,
That I may tell of all Your works.
—Psalm 73:25–28

Contents

I would like to thank Dolores and Trisha for their willingness to help during the editing process. Many thanks to my Family Life Group (small church group) for all your prayers. Last, but not least, thanks to Steve and Luke for your encouragement during this endeavor.

Introduction

The following are true (yes, true) stories that have occurred over the past thirty years or so. I never dreamed when many of them were happening that I would one day be telling them to others in the form of a book. I admit that I may not have every single detail exactly right because, quite honestly, I wasn't keeping a journal every time an event took place.

Many of my friends have heard me share at least some of these stories and have encouraged me to write them down. So here they are. I've had to change some names, as well as other specific identifying details to protect the innocent—or perhaps the guilty.

I trust the Lord will minister to you in some way; if not for just a laugh or two, or for a moment of thoughtfulness, but maybe during a time of thankfulness and appreciation of how he truly works in our lives.

18 — 30

Allen

Brent had a look of unbelief on his face.

Twenty-seven years earlier, I began my college career at Mercer University in Macon, Georgia.

I was a freshman. A freshman!

It was really exciting. On that first day, my mom and dad were on campus to send me off on the right track and wish me well. Shorter Dorm was my new home, and there were many new experiences for me to have: the proverbial dorm room, the unknown roommate, college classes, and countless other fellow students waiting to figure out what university life was all about.

In came the Allens—well, actually, Allen, Alan, Al(vie), and Jim (whose middle name is Allen).

Three of my soon-to-be friends were freshmen, and one was a senior.

We had a great time that year. We ate together,

rode around town, pulled pranks on each other—you get the picture. Our camaraderie was strong even though our backgrounds were diverse. A few of us were science majors, whereas the others were the more liberal-arts types.

As the college years went by, we continued to be tightknit and looked out for one another, even as our paths diverged (e.g., Jim had graduated) as we realized our gifts and callings. I knew I could ask for help anytime and they would be there for me as I was for them.

Four years went rather quickly, and the rest of us finally graduated, going our separate ways.

*

Life went on.

Many years passed (about twenty-five), and I started thinking about the fact that God, in his infinite wisdom, had surrounded me with the Allens. One day I decided to look up the name because, like the scripture says in Proverbs 22:1, "A good name is to be chosen above great riches." Well, interestingly enough, I discovered that the name Allen had several meanings. One in particular stood out. It meant "stone," and the deeper explanation that was given indicated that it was more of a small supporting rock or stone. It seemed as if the Lord had surrounded me with several supporting rocks as a source of strength, care, and hope during these very formative years of my adult life. I was encouraged by this, and I recognized that God truly knows what he is doing.

Always.

Back to Brent.

Brent is a friend who was my workout partner for years. He had moved from Miami to Titusville with his family for business purposes. Our friendship had grown, from just spotting each other on the weight bench to discussing issues related to work, family, politics, and you name it. We had even prayed together about certain situations.

One day at the gym, for some reason I felt I should tell Brent the Allen story. I told him how the Lord had surrounded me with Allens to help me in college.

As I went through the story, Brent got a look of

unbelief on his face. After I finished telling him the story, he looked at me and said, "My middle name is Allen."

Cool story, right?

Well, it's not over.

Years later another friend encouraged me to return to Mercer University. I had wanted to visit the school to see a place called the W. G. Lee Alumni House, a minimansion-sized residence on campus used to house university guests visiting from all over the world. I had lived and worked there as the caretaker for about a year and half during my sophomore and junior years. My boss at the time was the vice president of the office of development.

The school was on break when I contacted them for the visit, but a member of the office of development assured me they would set up a tour.

When I arrived for the visit, an associate vice president was there to greet me and show me around.

His name?

Allen.

Be Careful What You Ask For

Making a long story short, I had gone through some tough times in college, and God had brought me to a point of deeper understanding and power and trust in him. I really believed things in the Bible were true. For example, when Jesus says, "Ask and you shall receive," and "The pure in heart shall see God," he isn't kidding.

As I read the scriptures one day, I came across the verses in 1 Corinthians, chapter 12, that mention the gifts of the Holy Spirit. The whole Holy Spirit realization was interesting and exciting all in itself, even though I'd heard of the gifts before.

Oftentimes people are really keen on receiving the gift of speaking in tongues referenced in verse 10, but the one I became most interested in was the gift of distinguishing spirits. What exactly that was, I had no idea. Yet I was highly interested in receiving it, no matter what it meant.

So I prayed.

And I prayed.

And … I prayed.

For days I prayed, asking God for the gift of distinguishing spirits.

I really was clueless in my request.

Then, one day I was in the college cafeteria, eating dinner and minding my own business, when out of the blue a huge pain went through my stomach. I bent over briefly and then looked up.

Across the room was perhaps the prettiest woman on campus, staring at me.

It wasn't a look of attraction, though. The darkness in her eyes told a different story.

As she slowly, eerily turned away, I knew I'd had my first encounter.

Insulted

After graduating from college, I briefly returned home before moving to Florida to begin my life as a real, independent adult. A few years passed as I floundered around, trying to figure out a possible career direction for my life. Eventually a door was opened for me to work at the Cape Canaveral Air Force Station near Kennedy Space Center as a contractor to support various scientific endeavors of the National Aeronautics and Space Administration (NASA).

During my personal time away from the job, I was somewhat satisfied with life. For example, I believed that I was at a point in my individual journey with the Lord where I was becoming spiritually mature. I went to church, read the Bible, and tried to walk with God on a daily basis. Because of this, I considered my job on

Florida's Space Coast as an outreach of who I was in Christ. So when things went right (or wrong) with coworkers, I simply took it to mean God was doing a work and was trying to send me a message.

My occupation as a technician working in a laboratory for the space industry was average. It wasn't a glorious position, but I was gainfully employed. The money wasn't that lucrative, yet there was prestige found in the fact that I was supporting NASA in some way.

At the time, five other young adults were with me at a particular worksite. We each had our responsibilities and were attempting to do our best. As a Christian, I tried to set a good example in word and deed, and I think my coworkers knew this. That's why they were surprised when one day I departed from my customary behavior.

A colleague named Jacob often thought it was funny to cut people down—to insult and belittle them. Whatever made others feel bad was all right as long as Jacob felt on top in the end. I tried to handle his seemingly daily barbs and quips with the grace and excellence of a follower of Christ. But one morning, an insult of his hit me wrong, and I retorted with a comeback of my own. One of the other technicians in the lab was so surprised by my remark that he let out a big, "Ohhh!"

I couldn't believe the words had flown out of my mouth so quickly, yet a bigger issue occurred immediately. The Spirit of God let me know that I had done something wrong, and the conviction of my verbal sin was intense. From a worldly viewpoint, the guys were proud of me that I had given such a quick response to Jacob's condescending ways, yet the Holy Spirit wasn't.

But why?

The day went on, and I had soon forgotten about the incident.

God hadn't.

Nighttime fell, and I eventually made it to my bedroom.

It was prayer time, and I was in my routine. Pray a little. Read the Bible some. Fall asleep. When I got to the Bible part, the Lord had a message.

I have a habit of just opening up the Bible when I read. I usually don't plan on turning to any particular section; I let the pages lie where they may and see what God might be saying to me at any given moment. When I opened the Bible this time, I happened to turn to 1 Peter 3:9, which states, "Not returning evil for evil or insult for insult, but giving a blessing instead; for you were called for the very purpose that you might inherit a blessing."

mous, sympathetic, bbrotherly, ckind-hearted, and dhumble in spirit;
9 anot returning evil for evil or binsult for insult, but fgiving a cblessing instead; for dyou were called for the very purpose that you might einherit a blessing.
10 For,
    "aTHE ONE WHO DESIRES LIFE, TO LOVE
        AND SEE GOOD DAYS,

You've Got to Be Kidding

Secretly, we were waiting for the astronauts.

A coworker named Marty Richards was being given the Snoopy Award for his achievement in the field of chemical engineering as it related to the space program. He just didn't know it yet.

Our laboratory supervisor, Samuel, had gathered us in the laboratory's meeting room so Marty would receive the recognition while all his coworkers were present.

Samuel started the meeting as he had several times before by discussing laboratory business and operations, and then he spontaneously asked me to go up to the whiteboard to write something.

He never does that.

I did as Samuel requested and went to the board.

While standing there, I placed a marker in my

hand, waiting for his direction. Without warning, an interesting feeling overcame me, a sense that I was supposed to be there in front of people. Not just during the meeting that day … but something more.

The feeling left rather quickly and the meeting progressed. Eventually, the astronauts came in, and Marty got the surprising yet prestigious recognition he so deserved. There was much clapping for and praising of Marty in appreciation of his accomplishments. The astronauts finished their presentation, and the meeting ended soon after. Then our team of engineers and technicians returned to our usual, everyday research activities.

As time passed from days into years, I forgot about the whiteboard incident. I had switched jobs and, to be quite honest, was again directionless.

One day at church, someone (I don't remember if it was the pastor or another minister) was giving a teaching about the gifts and callings of God. We were asked to fill out a questionnaire, which would help us discover what the Lord might be leading us to do or perhaps had already gifted us in some way. One interesting aspect of the process was that we were to ask other people what they thought God's calling in our lives might be.

I followed along with the instructor's guidelines and finished the questionnaire. A few of my friends completed the portion that required the input of others. Their comments/observations were pretty much as expected.

All except for one. Mike suggested that I should become a teacher.

A teacher?

That's insane!

You see, I hate speaking in public. And I already had a job.

As time went by, I had either forgotten about the gifts/callings questionnaire or had simply shrugged it off. Either way, out of sight, out of mind.

Well, maybe not so fast.

Every once in a while, the idea of teaching would enter my thoughts. Just long enough for me to quickly consider it. Maybe talk about the possibility of becoming a teacher to a person or two.

Then, one day, another friend said he would

get me an application from the government so I could become a teacher. I hesitantly agreed to complete the form. I still wasn't so sure about the prospect of teaching. And with the government, who knows how long it would be before I was actually hired, if ever.

It took a while, but I eventually finished the application. Not knowing what the next step might be, or how long the process could last, I placed the application in the mailbox.

The next day, I got a call.

It wasn't from the government, though. It was from a church.

A staff member of a local church school called me and told me they were looking for a science teacher and as they prayed, my name had come to mind.

Really?

Wow!

I went in the interview and was called the next day. I was hired!

Within a week I was at the school preparing my room. Seven days later, students arrived.

Eventually, I became state certified and am currently a teacher in the public school system.

31 —40

I Will Protect You

All I wanted was some milk.

It was about ten o'clock at night, and this was unusual for me. I'm not a big milk fan, and like many single men, I didn't have any in the refrigerator that wasn't spoiled. This meant I would have to leave my apartment and go to the store. I can't remember the last time I'd thought about going out so late just to get something to drink.

I decided to go to the local Walmart for the milk. Getting up from the couch, I went through my kitchen and headed out the side door, closing it.

Once inside my car, I was ready to go. As I turned the car on and began to back out, an unfamiliar tune came on the radio. It started out like any other normal song. The music had a nice flow and steady beat, but the words quickly got my attention.

"Though the devil wants to kill you tonight, I will protect you."

Huh? What? I thought.

I had never heard such a song before, but … oddly … I sensed it was from the Lord. As I drove, I was a little in shock. I knew God was speaking to me, sending me a message through the song.

"Though the devil wants to kill you tonight, I will protect you.

"And you will know that it is I who saved you," the song continued, "because in the morning, when you wake up and look out the window, the sun will be shining, and the sky will be clear."

Hmmm. Okay.

While I continued driving, the singer went on to tell me that when the following night came along, the Lord would again protect me.

What was I to make of all this?

Was someone going to come out of the shadows and attempt to kill me?

Would there be a car accident?

Eventually, I made it to the Walmart and purchased the milk.

Then I drove home, parked the car, and returned to the apartment.

Getting out of the car, I walked to the stairs.

So far, I was safe.

I went up the steps.

No one attacked me.

I opened the door to the apartment.

I went through the kitchen to the hallway.

Then, I walked into my bedroom.

That's when I felt it …

… the change in the atmosphere.

It wasn't spooky.

It wasn't scary.

There was simply something *different* about the "feel" of the room.

Not knowing or understanding what this change, this feeling, meant, I decided to accept it for what it was and moved on through the bedroom.

Shortly afterward, I realized it was getting really late.

So

    I got ready

        and went to bed.

I don't even remember if I drank any of the milk.

Soon, I fell asleep.

Calmly.

Soundly.

Asleep.

                 *

Hours passed.

Then sometime in the middle of the night, it happened.

The violence woke me in an instant.

The winds outside were very loud, the torrents of air sounding as if they were going to tear my little home apart.

A prolonged outburst of an unexpected fury seemed to be ravaging the apartment complex.

Dazed by the sudden action, I didn't know what to think.

But then, almost as immediately as I had

awakened, I had this sense, an impression, that I was going to be okay.

And, surprisingly, I actually fell back asleep. Unharmed.

The sleep continued, uninterrupted.

The next morning, I woke to a phone call.

It was my mom, from more than four hundred miles away.

"Are you okay?" she asked in a panicked voice.

"Uh, yeah, sure," I replied. "Why?"

"Well, there was a tornado in Orlando last night, and I just wanted to make sure you were okay."

Orlando is in one county over from where I live.

I reassured her I was fine …

       I said my goodbyes and I love yous … that sort of thing …

   and hung up.

Then I turned to my window, pulled up the blinds, and looked outside.

It was sunny.

Not a cloud in the sky.

Then it hit me. The song!

I couldn't believe it.

As the day went on and turned into night, I returned to the bedroom.

That same sense filled the atmosphere.

Would God protect me again?

Of course.

The tornado on February 23, 1998, had been destructive and hurt many in the Orlando area.

For some unknown reason, God decided to save me from the devastation.

I am extremely thankful for his kindness and mercy.

A friend of mine, David, saw me one day about six months later. Without ever mentioning to him what had happened to me during the night, he said, "Did you know that the tornado that hit Orlando went directly over your apartment complex?"

Second-floor apartment where I was living.

Show Your Power

The trip to my hometown in Georgia from my current home in Central Florida is a long one. About seven hours.

Being single, I usually have to drive the trip by myself. There is no one to talk to or enjoy. It's just me, the road, scenery, and an occasional radio station that gets my attention.

This particular day was cloudy and overcast as I was riding down the highway in a farming area. It started to rain at about the same time a familiar song, "Show Your Power" by Kevin Prosch, came on the radio.

I began to sing along:

> He is the Lord, and he reigns on high
> He is the Lord

Spoke into the darkness, created the
light
He is the Lord

The rain got heavier, and the wind blew harder.
I sang louder:

Who is like unto him, never ending
in days
He is the Lord
And he comes in power when we call
on his name
He is the Lord

The rain continued growing in intensity, and
the wind blew with more fervor. I sang stronger
and with intensifying faith.

Show your power, oh Lord our God
Show your power, oh Lord our God,
our God

The rain had grown from just a whisper to a
loud, almost roaring freight train, with flashes
of lightning and crashes of thunder bombing me

with frightening blows that almost made me quit singing.

But I kept on—louder, yet afraid.

> Your gospel oh Lord is the hope of
> this nation
> You are the Lord
> It's the power of God for our salvation
> You are the Lord
> Show your power, oh Lord our God
> Show your power, oh Lord our God,
> our God

The storm continued to bombard me, but the presence of the Lord was unrelenting.

> We ask not for riches, but look to the
> cross
> You are the Lord
> And for our inheritance give us the
> lost
> You are the Lord
> Send your power, oh Lord our God

Send your power, oh Lord our God,
our God

As the song began to wind down, so did the storm. And when the music ended, so did the rain.

I Will Find You

I am no Liberace.

Seven months of piano lessons is about all I took, cumulatively.

Mine is a testimony of God using the weak ... really weak.

There was a period of time in my life where I would play the piano when I was a having a devotional/quiet time with the Lord. While praying, I would sit at the keyboard and play whatever song came to mind, songs of praise or worship that I sang at church or heard on the radio. Other times they would be songs I created.

It seemed to never fail that I would end up playing one particular made up song during almost every quiet time. I wondered why this was the case and thought perhaps there were words that might go with the song. They didn't come to mind, however (being a lyricist is not my forte).

Fast forward a few months.

One of my friends, a Methodist youth pastor, was riding his ten-speed bike when a dog seemingly came from nowhere and attacked him. He fell off the bicycle, injuring both arms. It took a while for him to recover. During the recuperation, he asked if I would be interested in going to an Episcopal retreat center with him so he could get away and pray. I agreed to go, knowing he would need help while he was there.

We traveled halfway across the state to get to the retreat center. The buildings and grounds looked peaceful and inviting, but ... having a Baptist background, I didn't know what to expect. Would we have to go around wearing robes and a hood? Could we speak?

It turns out it was not much different from a Baptist retreat center except for the log cabin-looking worship center. Inside were pews and a pulpit area, to the right a piano, and to the left a lot of candles (we don't do the candle thing where I attend church services).

My friend headed to the candles, and I went to the piano. As he prayed, I played the piano. You may think this was rude, and it probably was, but he had his side and I had mine.

As time progressed, something interesting happened. He stopped praying and walked over to the piano and said, "I think I'm getting words to your song."

I'd been playing the song, which had no lyrics. As he stood there and I played, the lyrics came out and a new song was born:

"I Will Find You," Lyrics and Music by C. Cantrell and R. Wilson

> Disappointed, brokenhearted,
> Lord, I've turned away again.
> I've stumbled beyond your will for me,
> Fallen into sin.
> And Lord, I'm so lost without you,
> Lord, my wounds are deep.
> Lord, I can't walk without you,
> Won't you come carry me?
> Chorus: (God Answers)

I will find you,
I will find you,
I will find you,
And carry you, carry you home.

Through the valley, I hear your cries,
They echo through the dark.
I'm not so far away from you,
Listen for my heart.
I myself will search for you,
Bind your wounds and make you
strong.
I'll reach down to where you are,
Carry you home where you belong.

Repeat chorus twice

Australia, Part A

Who doesn't like to travel?

Anyone?

Okay. I'm sure there are many of you out there who don't, but I'm just the opposite.

I will take a plane, walk onto a ship, hop onto a train, or anything else necessary to get out of town! Traveling around the country and the world is something I like to do.

But I hadn't really considered one particular country because it was so far away. It was ... Down Under.

Australia is many Americans' ideal, yet mysterious, vacation spot. Beautiful scenery, famous cities, the Great Barrier Reef, you name it.

But because of its distance from Florida, it usually didn't hold any prominent spot on the daily news or seldom came up in conversation. Oddly, though, that began to change.

I don't remember exactly what the first thing was, but I started to see Australia everywhere.

It may have been on a poster or on a billboard, but slowly, yet definitely, Australia began to show up on an almost daily basis. Steve Irwin (The Crocodile Hunter) was popular then, and his commercials and programming would catch my attention.

One day I distinctly remember watching what seemed to be program after program that either mentioned Australia or was directly related to Australia as I flipped from channel to channel on cable television.

Finally, one afternoon at a bookstore in Merritt Island, Florida, I realized a book I picked up sort of arbitrarily and absentmindedly had a big picture of Australia on the front cover.

My Australia awareness became so intense that I finally said to the Lord, "Okay, okay, I'll go to Australia."

Within what seemed like no time, a friend was able to get me in touch with a local pastor who used to minister there, and I connected with a missionary organization ministering to Islamic people in Australia. I would be the only American in the group.

As what seems to happen a lot with the Lord, if you agree to do what he wants, everything usually falls into place.

And that is what the case was here—except for just one tiny (or quite big, actually) problem. Money.

The lack of money was due to the fact that at the time I was a middle school teacher for a private Christian school. Finances were not abundant where salary was concerned.

But that doesn't matter if God *really* wants you to go somewhere. And he *definitely* wanted me to go.

Australia, Part B

The Lord really knows how to provide. It's just painful sometimes.

I was on my way home from my Family Life Group meeting in Titusville, Florida.

It was a simple drive. Just take a left onto Jackson Street and drive by the YCMA, and I'm almost there.

The YMCA ... hmmm. I love basketball. It was about 8:40 p.m. The Y closes at nine. That's plenty of time for any basketball enthusiast. I would have about twenty minutes to play my favorite game, if anyone else was available.

I quickly found a spot for my car and went inside. Sure enough, one more player was needed to play two-on-two.

Sign me up!

With little time to spare, we began to play. The game was fast-paced, competitive, and enjoyable.

As our friendly competition continued, one of the players took a shot at the goal and the ball hit the rim, bouncing up and hitting the backboard. I confidently jumped to grab the rebound and the fun stopped. One of the other guys had gone up for the basketball and got there right before me, snatching it before I could and, unfortunately for my face, elbowed me beneath my right eye as gravity pulled us back down to the court. The force of the impact was great, causing a long gash under my eye. The cut was quite extensive and appeared to be two to three inches long. Fortunately, an ambulance was not required, so I drove myself to the emergency room for repair.

After I arrived, an ER nurse told me I was fortunate the incident occurred when it did because their *best* plastic surgeon just happened to be on duty that night. Whew. When the doctor came in, he was able to stitch up the wound with precision and accuracy.

As time passed, the healing was so extensive that no one can tell I ever had a huge cut under my eye.

But that's not the big story. You see, I have hospital income insurance that gives me money when I experience a covered emergency or surgery. Because of my unexpected visit to the ER, I now had about $1,000 to put toward my mission trip to Australia. That was almost enough to cover the cost of the entire round-trip flight!

Weightless Wonder

About a year after my mission trip, I had an interesting experience.

I know most of us have probably seen the sight before—a jet flying high in the sky. Sometimes it's so high you don't see the contrail and can barely see the craft itself. Honestly, this isn't a new sight for me.

But …

One day when I looked up and saw a jet, I had the impression that somehow, someday, I would be working with aircraft.

You may think, *Well, what would be so odd about that?*

Nothing really, except that I had been told earlier by an FAA doctor that I would not be allowed to be a pilot due to a concern on my medical record. I had wanted to become an aviator but had been given the bad news that a pilot's license would not be granted under current guidelines. So the pilot dream was out of the question.

However, I'd had that impression, and I was pretty sure it was a message from the Lord. Therefore, this meant I would just have to wait and see.

Maybe a couple of months later I was headed back home after spending time at Playalinda Beach, which is located near Kennedy Space Center, Florida. I just so happened to look up and, once again, saw a jet flying high in the sky—and you guessed it—I felt a similar, if not the same, impression.

I didn't know what to think. Was I just imagining things, or was this thought, this impression, really from the Lord? I was unsure what to make of it and let it go.

A few more months went by. I was taking a class at a local college. I had become a public school teacher and was required to complete several courses before I could receive my permanent teaching certificate. (I had initially come from the private sector.)

This particular class was an all-day affair. During one of the breaks, I noticed that a fellow student was talking to the professor. After their discussion ended, I walked up to the student and asked her what they had been talking about.

How rude that must have seemed! Their conversation really was none of my business, and I couldn't believe I'd asked that question. It wasn't like me at all.

The student didn't even flinch and told me they were discussing the fact that her husband worked for an organization that was involved with a company that provided zero gravity flights to regular citizens, not just astronauts.

I was excited at the thought of a weightless flight and told her I would love to go sometime!

We finished our conversation and went our separate ways.

About two hours later she came back and said to me, "My husband just called and told me someone dropped from a flight. Would you like to go?"

Of course I would! Yes!

Not long afterward (maybe a month), I found

myself in a training class led by the Zero Gravity Corporation for the parabolic flight. Their Boeing 727 was to take off and fly along a path as if you are on a like a roller coaster, basically. Just like an astronaut in space, each passenger is able to float when the jet is at the top of the "hill" but is plastered against the floor due to extra gravity during the "valley" portion of the ride.

The flight was specifically given to teachers who would, hopefully, go back to their students after the flight was over and share the experience with them.

We were all excited and maybe a little nervous when we got on the plane. Amazingly, none of us became sick as we experienced varying degrees of weightlessness, such as lunar gravity, Martian gravity, and zero gravity.

The Zero Gravity Corporation staff were great and showed patient professionalism with all of us. After the flight was completed, we returned for a celebratory party. We ate, shared our experiences, took photographs, and then went our separate ways.

A few days after the flight, every teacher

received an email from Zero G. We were asked if we would be interested in working for the company on a part-time basis. If accepted, we would be Zero G coaches, like the people who were our group leaders on our inaugural flight.

I jumped at the chance. Who wouldn't want to be able to experience multiple zero g flights?

To my surprise, they hired me!

Over a period of about eight years, I flew at least forty zero gravity flights and I never grew tired of them. They were fun and exciting and I really enjoyed the people I met from all over the world.

The Lord was right when he impressed upon me that one day I would be working with jets. I just had no idea it was going to be like this!

Ghost Tale

It's hard being a ghost.

No one trusts you.

No one wants to be your friend.

No one believes you're real.

Everyone just stares.

I was forty-one years old—and a ghost. A credit ghost. I had lived my entire life and had never received a credit card. I didn't have a mortgage or a car payment. Some might think that was economic heaven. And it was, kind of. Except I didn't have some huge stash of cash lying around. My employment as a school teacher was anything but lucrative, and I'd reached that point in my life where I wanted to settle down. But no one wanted to help because I was not in the system.

One day, I went to a new bank to open an account and sat patiently as the banker entered my information. As I waited, he all of a sudden began to stare at me (or was it a glare?) as if I was some sort of imposter. There wasn't any information on me. I was nowhere to be found. Needless to say, credit was not extended.

JC Penney also had the chance to help me break into the credit system. Their denial was swift. Forty-one years old with no credit history? A card was denied.

No matter where I tried, the answer was always the same—no!

My car was gasping it last breaths, and I was desperate for a source of cash to get me through this transportation transition. Selling drugs for cash was out of the question. So was stealing. Where was I going to get the money? I had no real source of wealth to solve my money woes and nowhere to turn.

One Sunday morning I was at church. As usual, the singing was good and the sermon was relevant. How did God know I needed money?

That subject is seldom broached in our congregation. Usually it's a message or two in January or February and then we're on to other matters. Pastor Richard Lord spoke from Malachi 3:8–11, where God talks about being robbed in tithes and offerings. I had been faithful in giving tithes but not offerings.

God went on to say, "Bring the whole tithe into the storehouse, so that there may be food in my house, and test me now in this."

Really? You mean I need to give more money, now? I had heard the scripture before and even listened to messages pertaining to it too. But this time was different. I actually believed I was supposed to act on this directive from the Lord.

So I had a thought that went something like this: *Give $50 extra per paycheck.* Honestly, $50? But that's what came to mind.

To a rich person I realize this is probably nothing, but I was reaching my limit on giving.

Yet I gave.

And then God gave.

The more I gave, the more he gave.

Opportunities to purchase a car that I actually liked and wanted came up, and for some reason I finally got offered credit.

Then the government came up with a plan

where they would give first-time homebuyers $5,000 up front when they bought a home. I bought a home and got the five grand!

And slowly but surely, I was able to do renovations and get furniture to fill up the home. God is good!

Global Warming or Global Cooling?

Sometimes, you just don't know who to trust. The government says something, and because of its bad track record, you don't believe it. An organization may want money to further their cause, so they create statistics to coerce the masses into believing their hysteria.

Global warming seemed to be one of those cases.

Many of the scientific elite, who unfortunately give the appearance of hating or disbelieving in the existence of God, appeared to be totally engrossed in their belief that the world is going to be burning up very soon in an uncontrollable fashion just like the planet Venus appears to be doing at the moment.

But as a scientist who believes in a God that

really is in control, I smelled something fishy. It's like there is some hidden agenda, some unconfessed maneuvering behind all the clamor.

So I asked the Lord to do something in the beginning of the early stages of fall in 2009.

Please send a lot of cold weather.

In my heart, I think I just wanted enough cold to say to the global warming community that maybe they're wrong or they don't know everything, or something to that effect.

As autumn turned to winter, the weather in the nation began to show signs of cold, extreme cold in some cases. Even here in Florida, it seemed colder than usual.

I kept praying, though, believing God was going to do something with the weather.

At one point, when it started making national headlines, I actually told a worker at a local gym that I was praying for the cold to come.

It became so cold across the nation in February 2010 that it was believed to be the first instance snow was recorded in all fifty states at the same time (see i.gadling.com for more information).

Way to go, God!

Not everyone was happy about it, though.

On one of the chilly days here in Florida, I read an article or watched a report on the news about the cold, and it showed a picture of someone up north holding a sign that read "Please stop praying for snow."

Though I wasn't praying for snow, per se, I got the hint. I stopped praying for cold weather.

To Soccer or Not to Soccer

I'm a football player type. I loved playing tackle the man with the football when I was growing up and enjoyed juking around and through players when I had the ball. There's no greater fun for me.

Soccer, on the other hand, is also a sport I love to play.

Why on the other hand?

Well, I'm not so good at soccer. For the longest time, I was awful.

Awful.

I had played on an intramural team in college one year and didn't score a single goal. Actually, in the very last game we played, I scored a goal during the last few minutes of regulation. But the referee called it off because of an offside move I'd made. When I did take one last shot at the goal, it was blocked by the goalie.

Anyway, back to the story.

As the years went by, several friends were kind enough to let me play with their teams. It was fun, but the fact remained that I was terrible.

Then something happened. Things began to click. The game started to make sense. I properly dribbled the ball down the field. When someone kicked the ball my way, I learned to pass it strategically instead of acting as if it were a hot potato. My willingness to weave through several players to take a shot between the goal posts increased. I had arrived—or so I thought.

I had started playing soccer with some fellows in Cocoa, Florida, once a week for about a year. I was having fun and the camaraderie was good. They knew I didn't have the best of skills, but they accepted me for who I was, and, amazingly, the teams I played on would, more often than not, win. So I was happy with the fun I was having, and my little world was at peace.

Until "they" arrived. They were some fellows who I had played soccer with in the past. We had usually played against each other, and they were not exactly fond of my skills on the grass (of course, I wasn't that fond of my skills at that time, either).

But this was several years later.

For some reason, they seemed to have it out for me and were both vocal and nonvocal in their disdain. Their leering attitude was unmistakable.

What was I to do?

Well, at one point I almost got into a fight with one of them. He had "accidentally" hit me during a play, and I let him know in no uncertain terms that it would not happen again.

As time progressed, I grew weary of their behavior. I was unsure if I wanted to compete in such a negative environment, and I questioned whether I should stop coming to play with the group of regular fellows because of these other guys.

That wasn't the answer. Another one came to mind. Pray for them. Ask God to bless them.

Placing issues in the Lord's hands can make for some interesting outcomes.

When I saw them walking onto the field while people were warming up, I would pray.

A fascinating thing would happen.

As the game started, at least one of the offending men would almost get hurt immediately. Like a major sprained-ankle hurt.

One particular guy didn't show up for about four to six weeks after the first sprained ankle injury.

I didn't ask God to sprain his ankle. But it sure helped out with peace on the field.

Then the previously injured player came back. I prayed and asked God to bless him again.

Once we started playing that day, he suffered another leg injury. He was probably only out for three weeks this time.

I played soccer in Cocoa for maybe another month or two after that and then decided to focus on other athletic activities.

That's probably a good thing. Who knows how much God would have blessed the other players if they kept harboring ill will toward me?

God in the Rain

God in the rain. How wild is that?

Worshipping the Lord Jesus is an awesome experience. He is a God of love and great power and is so kind to us in many, many ways. One of those ways is during church services. With background music playing and a song leader vocally directing, the parishioner can be led into the presence of the Lord through praise and worship. The presence of the Lord is often gentle and peace-bearing. The comfort the Spirit of the Lord provides is genuine and greatly desired. There is really nothing like it.

So ...

One day I was at home minding my own business. I really don't remember what I was doing. It probably wasn't cleaning up the place or anything really eventful. I was just hanging out.

It began to rain.

The raindrops were just a sprinkle at first.

But almost immediately I started to sense it. It was the presence of the Lord.

As the rain increased, so did his presence.

Honestly, it felt great to be in the presence of the Lord. It always does.

As usual, the rain eventually ended and so too, it seemed, his presence.

This is not to say he isn't always there, but constantly sensing him is a different matter.

Here in Florida, it tends to rain a lot during the summer. It can be a daily occurrence. However, sensing God everyday was not the case.

Once again, though, about a month or so later, I was at home and it began to rain. Just like before, I started to sense the Lord's presence—the gentleness and peacefulness.

It was a surprise, as it usually seems to be, but welcome. Again, as the rain became stronger, so did the presence of the Lord. It's easy to rest when it's raining, especially if you're lying on a couch.

After this episode of rain/presence of the Lord,

I began to wonder. *Am I really sensing the Lord's presence? Am I just imagining things?*

Not too long after this occurrence of sensing the Lord, I came across the scripture in Psalm 68:8 that says, "the heavens dropped rain at the presence of God."

Wow.

God of the Coin Toss

He was really calm.

He walked into the classroom and stood beside me.

Maybe he just wanted to say farewell.

That wasn't it.

There was a problem. It was graduation day. He was a senior. Seniors are supposed to graduate.

At our school, seniors graduate about a week before everyone else completes the school year. That's fine, but as a teacher, you still have to finish teaching the remaining students.

When David walked in, he didn't want to say goodbye … he had an emergency. Though he was disrupting the class, I soon realized he would be taking precedence.

You see, David's school records were gone. Completely gone!

They couldn't be found. In this day of computer superiority and genius, his records, which I had updated frequently for my class, had somehow been deleted. But it wasn't just my class; it was all of his classes. David informed me that he had been personally sent down to find out what his grade should be by the staff member in charge of the computer records and that I was to do it immediately.

I don't always trust students. I did what any good teacher would do and began to see if what he was telling me was true. I got on the computer and went online to see if I could find his records. Amazingly, I pulled up the spreadsheet of the entire class, and sure enough, everyone's data was there but his.

I figured I would be able to determine what had gone wrong and recover his records. Maybe someone had inappropriately pressed a button, and because of my skills I would be able to simply restore what had been lost. I tried everything I could think of, but no keystroke would resurrect the thirty-five weeks' worth of David's grades. Finally, I gave in. I called the administrator, and she assured me she did not have his information and could not bring it back.

So what do I do? How should I handle this situation?

David probably had sixty grades or more for this semester alone, *and* they were grades that went through a weighting process I had used for years. I simply didn't have time to immediately recalculate what his true grade was, especially since I was still teaching.

I decided to ask the Lord for wisdom.

As I prayed, a neat thought came to mind. Do a coin toss.

A coin toss? To see whether the student graduates?

I could tell, just by briefly looking at his grades in my trusty hardbound grade book, that he hadn't failed my class. But grade point average (GPA) makes a difference too, so ...

I asked David how he felt about the option. Would he be willing to let his grade depend on the toss of a coin? Heads, he would get a C. Tails, a B.

David agreed.

With a toss of the coin, it spun in the air,

flipping and flopping, turning and spinning, and then, with a quick grasp, I turned it over and placed it on my wrist. It was tails!

David passed the class with the grade he needed to graduate! What a relief.

Final note: Once I had adequate time, I got out the calculator and officially verified that David actually finished with a B.

In the Middle of the Night

My sleep is usually sweet.

As I mentioned earlier, I often pray and read the Bible before I turn out the light. Many times the Lord takes these moments of communication to deal with me about the situations I faced during the day.

Did I fail to forgive someone?

Did I say something I shouldn't have?

Did I remember to put the laundry in the dryer?

Then I'm usually off to sleep.

After only four to six hours of rest, I may wake up. For some reason, this happens a lot.

It's not necessarily from some horrible dream. I just wake up. When this occurs, I may have more questions that go through my mind, such as: *Why am I awake? Should I be praying for someone or something?*

If I have no immediate direction and am at a point where I can't go back to sleep without delay, I can either lie in bed or get up.

Just lying in bed wears me out, so I've gotten to the point where I generally get up. I may go to the kitchen and eat, or get the ironing board out to iron, or grade papers (I am still a teacher).

Sometimes I even turn on the TV and watch something that will make me laugh. Laughter helps me a lot.

One night was a little different, though. Our country had been through 9/11, and our military was in Iraq and Afghanistan, actively looking for Osama bin Laden. No one seemed to know where he was. I certainly didn't know his location either, and the only thing I knew to do was pray. And that is what I did, not only for bin Laden, but for our involvement in the Middle East (the Lord knows my burden related to the situation).

This particular night I was woken from my slumber and, for some reason, went immediately to the television to turn it on. As the TV warmed up, it became quite clear that the news in the middle of the night was that bin Laden had just been found.

My prayer, along with probably countless other people's prayers, had been answered. The world could sleep a little easier. At least for one night.

Black-Eyed Blessing

He seemed to have a sneer. Or was it smirk?

Wallace was the proverbial talk-behind-your-back kind of person. Or, in this case, in front of you.

He didn't like me for some reason. Maybe it was because I stood for what was right. No matter his reasoning, as a teacher I believe that acting properly and responsibly in class is the appropriate student behavior.

Wallace appeared to be trying to drive a wedge between me and the other students, and in some cases, well, several, actually, was doing a good job of it.

Educators often dread these types of classroom behaviors. While other students are trying to gain knowledge and understanding, the misbehaving are busy manipulating circumstances, spreading rumors, and subverting the learning environment.

Wallace's attitude was becoming problematic.

Unsure of what to do, I fell back on the scripture that says to bless your enemies. In Romans 12:14, it says to bless those who persecute you; bless and do not curse. Later on, in verse 19, it says to leave room for the wrath of God, for it is written, "'Vengeance is mine, I will repay,' says the Lord."

So, that night, I did just that. I asked God to bless Wallace.

The prayer was nothing deep or profound. It was just a request of blessing.

When the next morning came, Wallace was in class ... with a black eye. And when he looked at me, there was a sense that he knew the reason he had gotten the black eye was in some unique way related to his negative behavior toward me.

Wallace's conduct was never a problem again.

Bonus Story: God Always Provides

I believe, when the Lord asks you to do something, he already has a plan in place and has the means for you to complete the request. The question we tend to ask often begins with "How?"

How do you expect me to leave my family?

How do you think I'm going to get the money?

How will I learn a foreign language?

How will I ever get the courage to face the consequences of obeying Christ?

How, how, *how*?

There are a lot of how's out there.

That's where I was in the summer of 2016. The Lord had called me to take two specific actions: first, write a book, and second, return to Australia.

The first activity, writing the book, made a lot of sense. Jesus has done so many things in my life that were obviously from him that it made sense to share the details with others to encourage believers in their walk with the Lord and nonbelievers to put their trust in him.

The second directive, traveling to Australia, did not initially come with specifics. I just knew he was asking me to go there again. Not knowing why I was being sent somewhere has actually turned out to be very exciting for me. Traveling under God's purpose can be quite rewarding, spiritually!

My only major issue with these requests was financial provision. I needed cash to travel to Australia and additional money to publish the book. Saving enough for either one alone seemed daunting. Life can be expensive, and I was living paycheck to paycheck, so the funding resource for these two adventures was not obvious.

This was my predicament that summer afternoon as I sat in the parking lot of the prayer chapel at Park Avenue Baptist Church in Titusville, Florida. I had come to the place in my life where I had no choice but to force myself to make a budget, to have a plan to reach these financial goals. As I headed inside the chapel, all I kept thinking was, *How am I going to do this? What can I do?*

I went inside to the foyer and then through the next door into the main room of the prayer chapel. It's quite spacious, and I found my way to the couch where I like to sit and pray (and sometimes sleep). I continued my thought process, basically like the broken record that is stuck playing the same music over and over.

How am I going to do this?

Where am I going to get the money?

As my mind wandered and looked at a sign on the wall that said "The Lord Our Provider," I had a clear impression from the Lord saying, "I will provide for you."

I immediately put my head down and began to think again. *How am I going to do this? What am I going to do?* Pondering my fiscal quandary, my eyes again found the "The Lord Our Provider" sign, and to my surprise, the Lord reminded me that he was going to provide for me.

Again, I instantly put my head down and

began to think, *How am I going to do this? What am I going to do?*

Somehow, it finally dawned on me that if God has said he is going to provide for me, then *he* will be the one who gets me the money. It would be up to him, not me.

I stayed inside a little longer and then decided to leave. Making my way out of the chapel, I went back to my car. I started the vehicle and began to head home. While driving, I received a phone call from someone unexpected—a secretary for an attorney who had a surprise for me. I was to receive some money.

"How much will I be receiving?" I asked.

She didn't know the exact number yet, but she promised that she would call me back when she determined the exact value.

About thirty minutes later she called and advised me of the amount. It was enough to cover both the trip to Australia and the publishing of this book.

The Lord *is* my provider.

Final Word

I hope you have enjoyed these short stories. Each one is a snapshot of what God has been doing in my life and what he can do in yours.

If you would like to contact me regarding the book or perhaps share one of your own experiences, please use the following email address: chriscantrell2020@outlook.com.

About the Author

Chris Cantrell has been a Christian since childhood, and for over forty years he has had many opportunities to see God at work in his life, his friends' lives, and in our nation. His strong belief that there really is a God has enabled him to navigate life's many trials. Through direct intervention from a holy Lord, this science teacher has been delivered from death, received personal information about people he's just met, and been given divine wisdom on the job.

CPSIA information can be obtained
at www.ICGtesting.com
Printed in the USA
LVHW112044161118
597207LV00001B/59/P